Acknowledgments

FRONT COVER © Edith Widder/ORCA; **BACK COVER** (t/l) © sciencepics, (b/l) © Edith Widder/ORCA, (b/r) © David Fleetham, Visuals Unlimited Inc./Science Photo Library; **INSIDE FRONT COVER** © David Fleetham, Visuals Unlimited Inc./Science Photo Library; **PAGE 1** © Edith Widder/ORCA; **PAGES 2–3** (t/l) © British Antarctic Survey/Science Photo Library, (b/l) © Dr. Morley Read/Science Photo Library, (r) © David Wrobel, Visuals Unlimited Inc./Science Photo Library; **PAGES 4–5** Solvin Zankl, Visuals Unlimited Inc./Science Photo Library; **PAGES 6–7** © Wim Van Egmond, Visuals Unlimited Inc./Science Photo Library; **PAGES 8–9** (bg) © KPG_Payless, (l) © Terry Priest Art Farmer @ flickr, (r) © Cathy Keifer; **PAGES 10–11** © Dr. Morley Read; **PAGES 12–13** Edith Widder/ORCA; **PAGES 14–15** © Edith Widder/ORCA; **PAGES 16–17** Edith Widder/ORCA; **PAGES 18–19** © Dante Fenolio/Science Photo Library; **PAGE 20–21** © Will Ho; **PAGES 22–23** © Dante Fenolio/Science Photo Library; **PAGES 24–25** © David Fleetham, Visuals Unlimited Inc./Science Photo Library **PAGES 26–27** © Edith Widder/ORCA; **PAGES 28–29** © Edith Widder/ORCA; **PAGES 30–31** © Edith Widder/ORCA; **PAGES 32–33** © Edith Widder/ORCA; **PAGES 34–35** © Edith Widder/ORCA; **PAGES 36–37** © Edith Widder/ORCA; **PAGES 38–39** © Edith Widder/ORCA; **PAGES 40–41** © Edith Widder/ORCA; **PAGES 42–43** © Edith Widder/ORCA; **PAGE 44–45** © Edith Widder/ORCA; **PAGES 46–47** © Richard A. McMillin; **PAGE 48** © Brian Brake/Science Photo Library.
Used under licence from Shutterstock.com

Key: bg = background, t = top, b = bottom, c = center, l = left, r = right.
ORCA = Ocean Research & Conservation Association

Way to Glow!

Amazing Creatures That Light Up in the Dark

Written by Lisa Regan
Developed & Published by Red Bird Publishing Ltd., U.K.
Original Glow Art and Production by Red Bird Publishing Ltd., U.K.

This edition published by Scholastic Inc., 557 Broadway, New York, NY 10012, by arrangement with Red Bird Publishing Ltd.

SCHOLASTIC and associated logos are trademarks and/or registered trademarks of Scholastic Inc.

ISBN: 978-0-545-90661-6

COPYRIGHT © 2016
Red Bird Publishing Ltd., U.K.   www.red-bird.co.uk

10 9 8 7 6 5 4 3 2 1   16 17 18 19 20
Printed in Heshan, China

Contents

Lights-Out!

Our world is a wonderful place, full of beautiful sights and amazing creatures.

When the lights go out, a whole new world comes to life: creatures that **glow, and flash, and sparkle.** Some creatures can even create their own light! This is called **bioluminescence,** and it is a **chemical reaction** caused by special substances mixing together within the creature's own body.

Read on to learn more about this awesome **phenomenon,** and turn out the lights for a cool look at some glowing displays.

Prepare to be blown away by nature!

When you see a ☆, hold the book under a light source for thirty seconds. Then turn off the lights to see the pages glow!

Hatchetfish

A hatchetfish is extremely thin if you look at it from the front. This gives it its name: It looks like the blade of a hatchet, which is a type of small ax.

This **amazing creature** spends its whole life in the deepest parts of the ocean. It is small enough to fit in your hand. Its eyes point upward so it can see potential **prey** swimming overhead. Anything that moves above it will appear as a dark **silhouette** against the light at the water's surface.

The hatchetfish is smart, too. It uses bioluminescent light on its sides to prevent its own body showing up in the same way. This is called **counterillumination** and is a smart way for the hatchetfish to stay hidden. It's like an **invisibility cloak** for fish!

Dragonfish

Let's meet another cool creature that *lurks in the deep oceans.* The dragonfish has a long, dangling **barbel** under its chin with a *blue light* on the end, which the fish can *flash on and off.* The light acts like bait on the end of a fishing line, attracting creatures for a closer look.

DID YOU KNOW?

Dragonfish teeth are so long that the fish can't close its mouth around them! The teeth can fold back into its mouth while the dragonfish eats.

The dragonfish is shorter than your forearm, but it can eat big prey because its jaws are very **flexible.** It can also create its own *red light,* which allows it to see but not be **detected** by the many ocean creatures that can see only blue light.

7

Firefly

These insects are unusual, since bioluminescent creatures normally live in the sea, not on land. Fireflies are a type of beetle and are sometimes called *lightning bugs.* Their **larvae** also give off light and are nicknamed glowworms (see page 48).

The adults, which are only about the size of a human's fingernail, eat nectar and pollen from flowers. Their *flashing lights* may be used to attract a **mate.** You are most likely to spot a firefly at **dusk** or during the night.

DID YOU KNOW?

Fireflies can produce different shades of light, from pale red to yellow and green. They can flash signals or give off a steady glow.

Click Beetle

These long, skinny beetles have a neat trick to get them out of trouble. When they **sense danger,** they snap the front sections of their body together, making a loud **CLICK** that scares away **predators.** They can use the clicking action to flip over, too, if they get tipped onto their back.

DID YOU KNOW?

A click beetle cannot flash, it can only glow. But it can make its light glow brighter if it is being bothered by a predator.

Some click beetle species have another way to protect themselves: They have two bioluminescent dots on the front part of their body and a light on their underside. These lights signal that the beetle makes a *nasty meal.* Predators, beware!

Anglerfish

This crazy creature is not going to win any prizes for its looks, but that doesn't matter, since it lives in the **darkest parts of the ocean.** It has a bioluminescent **lure** above its large mouth to attract prey, which the anglerfish then **gobbles up.**

This picture shows a female anglerfish. The male is tiny and lives a very strange life. He attaches himself to the female's underside and feeds off her blood. Eventually, the male's eyes and body **disappear,** and all that remains are the parts of him that the female needs to produce babies.

DID YOU KNOW?

The anglerfish has such a stretchy mouth and body that it can eat prey up to twice its own size!

Jellyfish

Jellyfish are an excellent example of the sea creatures that typically use bioluminescence, for several reasons. They use the light to attract a mate, to draw in prey, and to *scare off any predators.*

DID YOU KNOW?

Jellyfish have lived in the oceans for millions of years. They were swimming around long before the dinosaurs arrived!

Jellyfish are mostly made up of water and do not have a brain. Actually, they don't have many body parts at all: *no blood, no bones, no heart, and no lungs!*

Plankton

There are lots of **tiny creatures** in the ocean that
are too small or weak to swim against the current.
As a group, they are known as **plankton.**
The worm shown here is one of them,
and its proper name is *Tomopteris*.

When it glows, only the outline
of the plankton is visible.

Its body is usually **transparent,** but it can still give off its own light. Some make blue light, while others make yellow light. They are *smaller than your finger,* although some have a long, rippling tail.

Eye-Flash Squid

This little beauty is the length of your thumb but has around **550 tiny dots** on its body that light up with bioluminescence. It also has lights below its large eyes, giving it its name.

The lights can be flashed in patterns to confuse its enemies or to make its body match the light coming from above. This *sneaky creature* senses how warm the water is and changes its lights from *green to blue* as the water gets colder or is lit by the moon.

Glowing Ocean

This ocean glow is a truly awesome sight! Waves breaking on the beach cause carpets of light, and a person walking along the shore can leave **glow-in-the-dark** footprints. This is actually bioluminescent plankton that glows when it is disturbed.

Scientists are unsure why it gives off this glow, although it may be to stop creatures from eating it. Plankton can exist in huge patches, called blooms, which look pinkish red in the daytime and can make the water **poisonous** to other creatures.

DID YOU KNOW?

The Indian Ocean is famous for its milky seas, which glow blue white as ships cut through the waves, disturbing the plankton, and leave trails of light behind them.

Flashlight Fish

For a light-producing fish, this one is unusual because it lives in much shallower waters. It has a **bean-shaped light** under its eyes that is a very bright white—possibly the **brightest of any glowing creature.**

The flashlight fish's light **glows constantly.** However, the fish can make the light seem to flash on and off by flipping it over so it is hidden. The fish usually does this two or three times each minute, but if it is in **danger,** it can flash its light every second!

DID YOU KNOW?

Some sailors follow the lights of these fish to help guide their boats through coral reefs at night.

23

Bobtail Squid

The bobtail squid is a tiny creature that is only the length of your thumb and uses light to hide itself while it hunts at night. Its body has a light organ that is home to bioluminescent **bacteria,** which feed on sugars produced by the squid. In return, the bacteria *glow to match the moonlight* above the water.

The squid gets rid of the bacteria every day and reloads with new bacteria to light its way the next night. One species of bobtail squid is nicknamed the *fire shooter* because it squirts a cloud of light to confuse its predators.

DID YOU KNOW?

Bobtail squid have been sent into space to study what happens to the bacteria when there is less gravity (the force that keeps us anchored to the ground on Earth).

25

Sea Pen

The long, thin creature shown here is a sea pen, and it is being attacked by a sea star. Sea pens give off a **bright green light** when they are touched or disturbed, which you can see in the small photo below. They usually stick up from the ocean floor like plants. Sea pens can suck in water to make themselves bigger.

Some sea stars can also glow. When a sea star is under attack, it throws off one of its arms, which floats away. The predator follows the light from the glowing arm and leaves the sea star alone.

Many sea pens have *feathered sides* and look like old-fashioned quill pens. They are made up of several creatures called polyps that resemble *sea anemones.* One polyp makes up the long stalk and a bulb holds it in place. The other polyps form the quill feathers.

Helmet Jellyfish

This creature may look red to you, but in the dark oceans, it will seem black and *almost invisible.* However, it can produce flashes of blue light, shown in the picture below, to warn predators that it is *not safe to eat*.

The helmet jellyfish lives in *deep oceans* but is also found in some Norwegian fjords (lakes), where it is crowding out the fish that live there. It eats both plankton and small fish, which are hidden inside the jellyfish's red stomach until they can be digested. That way, they do not give away the jellyfish's location.

DID YOU KNOW?

Light is harmful to these jellyfish, so they live in deep water and only come closer to the surface at night.

29

Comb Jelly

Comb jellies are similar to jellyfish but have rows of plates that work like oars to move the creatures through the water. Some comb jellies are as *big as a football,* but others are tiny. They have a blobby, see-through body that *shimmers* even when they don't produce bioluminescent light.

DID YOU KNOW?

One type of comb jelly has long, sticky tentacles for catching food. It is round with hairs on its outside and is nicknamed the sea gooseberry. Don't try to eat it, though!

Their bioluminescence is blue and it's used to *scare away predators.* Some jellies use it for flashing warning lights, while others release *glowing clouds* to blind their attackers.

Krill

These small, shrimplike creatures are no bigger than your pinky finger, but the oceans contain **millions** of them. They are one of the most important foods for many sea animals, from fish to whales.

Krill are sometimes nicknamed *light shrimp* because they produce their own bioluminescent light. They use it to hide against the pale surface of the water. Certain types of krill are so smart that they can dim their light if a cloud covers the sun, and brighten it again when the cloud has passed!

DID YOU KNOW?

Krill have lights on the end of their eyestalks as well as on different parts of their body.

Octopus

There are hardly any bioluminescent octopuses, but this one has adapted some of its suckers to give off light. Its body is reddish brown, but its arms have blue-green lights that flash on and off in a *twinkling, circular pattern.*

Like other glowing creatures, this octopus probably uses its lights to defend itself against predators and to attract food to eat. It has **eight arms,** like other octopuses, but its arms are covered by a balloon of skin.

DID YOU KNOW?

Non-bioluminescent octopuses are masters of disguise: They can change the color of their skin to blend into the background.

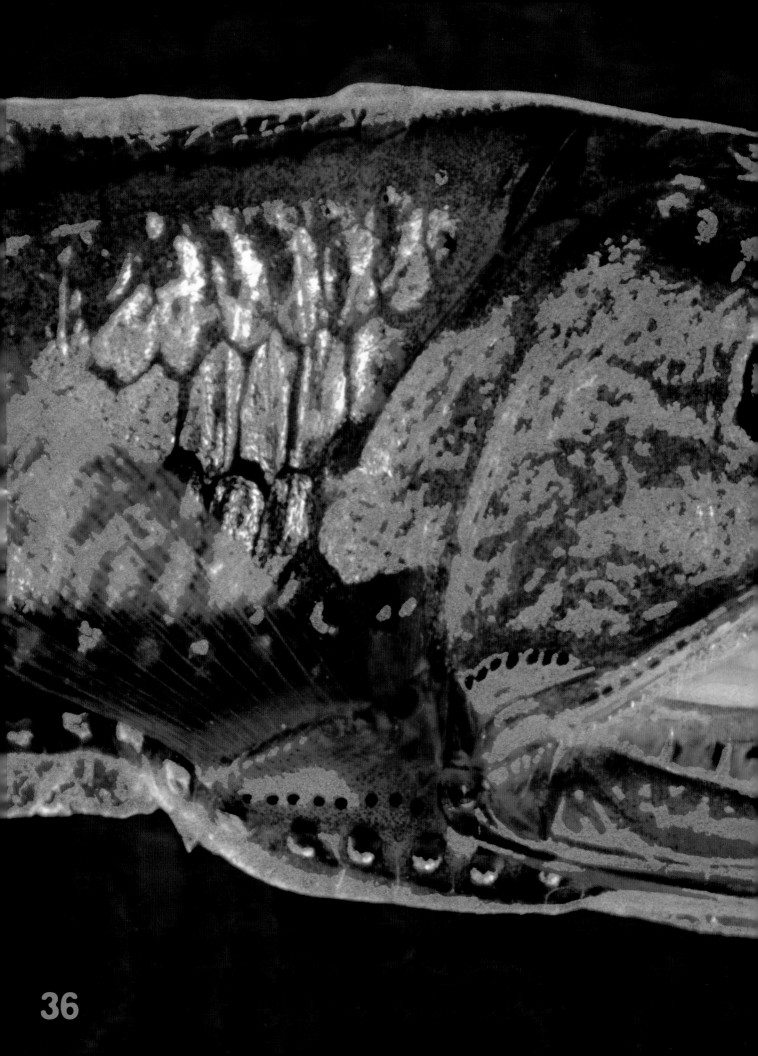

Viperfish

Let's meet another deep-sea creature that goes fishing with a *light-up lure*. The viperfish has a long barbel on its back that it dangles near its mouth. This tempts other fish to swim close enough for the viperfish to *gobble them up*.

DID YOU KNOW?

The viperfish has a stomach that can grow larger if there happens to be a lot of food around. It is a built-in storage closet!

This fish is covered nearly everywhere in lights. They are on its body, its fins, its head, and even *inside its mouth and its eyeballs!*

37

Siphonophore

Siphonophores are long clear creatures that belong to the same family as *jellyfish, corals, and anemones.* Each one is made up of lots of smaller animals fastened together. To catch food, they have *stinging tentacles,* which are hidden inside a red stomach.

When disturbed, siphonophores give off a *green or blue glow.* They are difficult to catch and study because their gooey bodies are very delicate. One of the most famous, and dangerous, is the *Portuguese man-of-war,* which can give a painful sting even after it has died!

DID YOU KNOW?

Siphonophores can be one of the longest animals in the world. Some are even longer than a blue whale!

Decapod Shrimp

Here's another creature that **squirts out light!** The decapod shrimp is bright red, but since red light cannot be seen in the ocean depths, its body is **almost invisible** to predators.

DID YOU KNOW?

The decapod shrimp is nicknamed the fire-breathing shrimp, although the light can come out of other parts of its body, not just its mouth.

However, if something does get too close, this creature has a clever getaway plan. It squirts out a **shining blue cloud,** and while its attacker is confused, the shrimp **backflips to safety!**

The squid's red body is covered with darker dots, called **photophores,** that produce light. Its body glows with brilliant, glimmering shades of blue and green, earning it the nickname *"jewel squid."*

DID YOU KNOW?

Scientists think the squid's yellow eye is used to spot sneaky creatures trying to hide with counterillumination, since it cancels out the effect of their blue lights.

43

Atolla Jellyfish

This deep-sea creature uses its bioluminescence as a kind of **burglar alarm** to defend itself. By flashing its lights when it is under attack, it attracts the attention of larger predators that scare away, or simply eat, its attacker. This leaves the jellyfish free to sneak away.

The blue circle you see in the small picture below is the ring of lights, not the jellyfish itself, which is red. The lights flash around and around in a circle, like a *spinning pinwheel.* It is an amazing sight!

Lanternfish

It is hard to believe, but this creature is possibly the **most common fish** in all of the world's oceans. You will probably never see one, though, because they live in deep water until nighttime, when they swim up to feed on plankton closer to the surface.

Lanternfish have a line of lights down each side of their body. They probably use their lights to attract a mate.

The surface is a **dangerous place** for lanternfish because they are a popular food for all sorts of creatures, including squid, penguins, whales, sharks, and seabirds. Although the body of the lanternfish is covered in **silvery scales,** it can give off its own light. Some make blue light, while others make green or yellow light.

47

Glowworm

The term "glowworm" can be used to describe many different types of bioluminescent insect larvae. The sparkle pictured here is produced by the larvae of fireflies (see page 8). They twinkle to warn potential predators that they **taste really bad!**

Some caves in Australia and New Zealand light up with the glow from the **fungus gnat.** This is another kind of fly larva that uses bioluminescence. Its light is designed to attract prey into sticky webs.

DID YOU KNOW?

In World War I, soldiers collected glowworms to give them light in the dark trenches.

Glossary

bacteria	tiny living things that are too small to see
barbel	a long "feeler" for sensing things
bioluminescence	the ability of some creatures to produce their own light
chemical reaction	making a new substance from two or more substances; light or heat can be given off during the reaction
counterillumination	using light to hide against the bright background at the surface of the ocean
detect	to notice or discover
dusk	the time when day turns into night
flexible	bendy or stretchy
larva (plural = larvae)	an insect after it hatches from an egg but before it becomes an adult; also known as "grub"
lure	bait used to attract fish or other creatures
mate	a partner for producing babies
phenomenon (plural = phenomena)	an unusual or special situation
photophores	spots on a creature's body that give off light
plankton	a mixture of tiny plants and animals that float in the ocean
predator	an animal that hunts other creatures for food
prey	an animal that is hunted and eaten by other creatures
silhouette	a dark outline against a light background
transparent	see-through